THREE WISE MOMS

OUR LESSONS, YOUR LIFE

Written By:
Many Moms With One Heart

Three Wise Moms — 1st ed.
ISBN 978-0-9998755-0-6

This book is dedicated to our brave, bold, and beautiful daughters, Arwa, Jocie, and Shelby.

Thanks and recognition to all of those who have contributed to the heart of the book...

Connie Cooper Shepherd – Conceptual Author

Mary Chevaz – Editor
Rachel Wright – Editor

Mom Contributors:
Aisha Jumaan
Catherine Cooper Garrett
Connie Cooper Shepherd
Gina Maria Keene
Jay Eveland
Jenny Taylor
Joyce McAnany
Karen McAnany Hatcher
Mary Groth Jacobs
Mary Kay Brown
Missy Shepherd
Natalie Thomson
Rachel Wright
Sharin Porter Nelson

TABLE OF CONTENTS

FOREWORD

This book is an extraordinary gift from the depths of the hearts of women who have garnered keen insights into living purposefully and meaningfully. Written by wise and compassionate women, the book is a guide for living with grace and peace in the midst of challenging times. Keep it close at hand regardless of circumstances in your life and in our world today. In the words of Albert Camus: "Real generosity toward the future lies in giving all to the present." Though written for children on the verge of adulthood, it's a treasure trove for anyone seeking to make sense of their lives at any age. Each page is embedded with pearls for contemplation based upon the hard-won wisdom of experience. In today's world of turbulence and uncertainty, we need to demonstrate our capacity to be kind, compassionate, and humane. The Three Wise Moms remind us that we are not alone; their stories provide solace during difficult times and direction for the future. Remember to dip into the book anytime you need encouragement to keep going. Within these pages you'll find answers to questions you may not even have articulated! The Wise Moms write with experience, integrity, and genuine heart. Read their words to maintain hope regardless of your daily difficulties, and share it with others so they too can benefit.

Geri Marr Burdman, Ph.D.

Author of *Search for Significance*

PREFACE

One thing is evident, the world needs healing. We see the division in politics and in race relations. We see the harm being done to our planet through human-made climate change leading to the sea level rising and unprecedented weather patterns. Off the news, we see how our children and our friends' children deal with the FOMO (fear of missing out) anxiety produced by social media and its fabricated perfection, and the sense of anonymity this new world of communication has created. Deep down many of us are struggling to find peace in our hearts, whether we are conscious of it or not. In honest moments, we convey to each other that there must be something more than "bigger is better" or material wealth.

It was in one such honest moment that the idea for this book was born. Three friends, each with a teenage daughter, and all from diverse backgrounds, came together with an idea to share the wisdom and lessons each had learned in her life. They wanted their daughters to have a written compass they could take with them as they began the next phase of their life journey – something timeless, while hopefully reminding their young hearts and minds that they were loved, precious, never alone, but also that they each had a responsibility to contribute positively to the world with the gifts each had been given.

On the one hand, finding one's life purpose is a profoundly daunting task. On the other, it is simple if taken a step at a time, a day at a time. If we each go about our business in a way that is mindful and builds true connection with each other and our world, positive results are inevitable. The three friends wanted to remind their girls and boys that life's journey was about creating meaning, not perfection. Their dream was that their children would prosper, find love, know happiness, and make a difference in our world.

Inspired by the spirit of one step at a time, these moms wrote encouraging messages and words to live by. Their entries are principles and lessons learned throughout their lives and in the lives of other contributing moms. They can be read daily or anytime throughout the year for encouragement and are reminders about the uniqueness and beauty of each living thing. The moms have also included open reflection pages for their children to capture their own thoughts. Reflection leads to learning, which leads to action with wisdom.

They named the book, "Three Wise Moms." As their friendship developed and they shared their stories, it became clear that while they had come from various backgrounds, they had the same hopes and wishes for their children. These moms had experienced birth, death, divorce, war, relocation, poverty, immigration, and many of the circumstances, struggles, and life experiences had contributed toward rich, textured lives. Each of them wanted their children to know how important their choices were in life, yet also how truly loved they were.

Aisha is a public health professional and is currently managing health projects in her birth country, Yemen. She obtained her undergraduate and graduate degrees from Mills College (BA), Emory University (MPH), and UNC-Chapel Hill (PhD). Aisha has worked in national and international public health programs, including the CDC, UNFPA, and PATH. She also taught at Emory University in Atlanta and Sana'a University in Yemen. Aisha loves being a daughter, sister, wife, and mom. She loves to cook, entertain diverse groups, and work with interfaith communities to build bridges.

Connie is a mom, sister, friend, and recognized marketing professional who has held executive leadership positions at P&G, Kellogg, Hershey, and Starbucks. Currently, Connie is the CEO and President of a successful consulting company, Cooper Consulting, LLC. She is known as an inspirational leader and change agent having pioneered entrepreneurial business opportunities and built innovative approaches to new markets. Connie's faith has been her guiding compass in life and the foundation of her mission to make a difference for good. Connie loves God, cold beer, country music, and laughing out loud.

Natalie is an educator, entrepreneur, and is currently a city planner. She has an undergraduate degree in business administration with honors, and graduate degrees in elementary education and child and family studies. She has worked in both the private and public sectors and has done consulting for government agencies. Natalie's favorite roles are as wife and mother. She loves to dance, cook, and drink iced tea in the sunshine.

May you have the courage to pursue your dreams one step at a time, the compassion to reach out to others on your journey, and the wisdom to make your choices count.

ACCEPTANCE

"O mankind, we have created you from male and female and made you into nations and tribes that you may know one another." Quran 49:13

In a world that has become connected and interconnected with people traveling from one continent to another within hours, many of us are confronted with people who have different religious beliefs, cultures, languages, gender, and cultural norms. Our children's world is even more connected than ours, and they are more likely to encounter people who are different. My hope is that we teach our children to accept and respect these differences instead of judging others and creating animosity.

When my daughter was about two to four years old, I used to volunteer at a homeless shelter for women and children. I would take her with me and observe with amazement how she and the children in the shelter played together in harmony. It reminded me that our prejudices are learned behavior. Another time, we hosted a group of refugee children from different countries who spoke different languages, yet they still were able to play together well. As my daughter was getting older, I dreaded the fact that she would start paying more attention to the differences that she had been oblivious to.

A Muslim philosopher once said, "There are as many paths to God as there are human souls." There are differences between faiths but also differences within faiths and how members of the same family decide to practice their devotion to God. Given these infinite ways to be one with God, who has the right to determine the "right path"? No one!

Another Muslim philosopher wrote that all people are descendants of Adam, who became alive when God breathed into him. Therefore, we all have inherited God's breath, and we are all sacred.

I sincerely believe that if the founders of the faiths that people profess to today were resurrected, they would be appalled by how exclusionary their teachings have become. I also believe that if they tried to correct the prejudices that people attribute to their faiths, that they would be persecuted by the most ardent followers of the religion.

When we accept the differences of others without judgment, we can live freely and in peace with ourselves and with one another. My dream is to have acceptance be the norm instead of tolerance. That would be a sign of a strength in who we are, in our beliefs, and an acknowledgment that we all reach God in a personal way. My wish is to be able to pray the way I want in any "House of God" anywhere. My favorite places of worship are "meditation/ prayer" rooms at airports. There I can perform an Islamic prayer with people of other faiths praying in their own way next to me. It is then that I feel that we are all one with God.

Mom Aisha

YOUR THOUGHTS

ADD VALUE

Seek to add value in as many circumstances as possible. Add value to your relationships by being a good listener. Add value to your soccer team by going to practice every day, working hard, doing your best in each play in which you are involved. Add value to your school community by taking on leadership or support positions as you can. Add value to your home by caring for your family and participating in the daily activities that keep the household running, like cleaning up, cooking, caring for one another, laughing.

Eventually you will add value to your own home and workplace. You will become a team player who can be counted on to be reliable and to bring your skills and to constantly grow in ways that add value to any project or situation.

There will be times that you cannot add value. Either the work or circumstances will be too difficult. At that point, you must decide if you want to acquire the skills and knowledge it takes or get the help you need to eventually add value to the situation. In this case, your investment of time and learning will be well worth it. If you don't believe that you are adding value, this is valuable information, too. It means that the situation or work is not a good fit. You then have another decision point.

Most importantly, seek to add value to your relationships. Our world needs more people who know how to connect and add value to relationships.

I'd like you to envision a world where all or most are adding value. We are adding energy to our families. We are adding value to customer service experiences. We are adding nutritious value to what we eat. We are adding value to students' educational experiences to learn what is useful in life. If you seek to add value for others, you will ultimately add value to your own life.

Mom Natalie

Book: *Seven Habits of Highly Effective People*
by Stephen Covey

YOUR THOUGHTS

ATTITUDE

"Do not be anxious about anything, but in every situation, by prayer and petition, with thanksgiving, present your requests to God. And the peace of God, which transcends all understanding, will guard your hearts and your minds in Christ Jesus." Philippians 4:6-7

ATTITUDE is everything! Let's be grateful for the things God has given us and have a wonderful day! Oftentimes, we just need a reminder of the numerous blessings in our lives. Most of the things we are worried about today, we won't even remember next week.

The person who believes they can do something is probably right – so is the person who believes they can't.

With so much craziness going on in this world, sometimes it's hard to look at the bright side and be positive. I came across this cute little story and thought you might get a chuckle out of it.

There once was a woman who woke up one morning, looked in the mirror, and saw that she had only three hairs on her head. "Great," she said, "I think I'll braid my hair today."

So she did and had a wonderful day.

The next day she woke up, looked in the mirror, and saw that she had only two hairs on her head. "Hmm," she said, "I guess I'll part my hair down the middle."

So she did and had a wonderful day.

The next day she woke up, looked in the mirror and saw that she had only one hair left on her head. "Wow," she said, "today I get to wear my hair in a ponytail."

So she did and had a wonderful, wonderful day.

The next day she woke up, looked in the mirror, and saw that there wasn't a single hair on her head.

"Thank God!" she exclaimed. "I was running out of things to do with my hair!"

Mom Mary

YOUR THOUGHTS

AUTHENTICITY

"We have to dare to be ourselves, however frightening or strange that self may prove to be." May Sarton

We live in a world filled with advertising, magazines, TV shows, and movies telling us what to look like, how to behave, what is normal, and what is "cool." Moreover, social media, is filled with images, capturing seconds of a person's life that defines for us new and unrealistic norms whether that is in appearance, body figure, clothing, makeup, or other factors that distort the true image of the individual. We experience strong pressure to conform to these new norms, and it becomes very difficult for younger children to be true to themselves. Therefore, we must insist that all we reach into our hearts and learn the skills to be authentic for physical and mental wellbeing.

I was at a dentist office once, when my daughter was in elementary school, and picked up a magazine called "Sixteen." I read an article that was very disturbing. The author offered advice to young girls on how to please their boyfriends' male friends. She advised bringing food, talking less, looking good, and engaging in their activities. In the same issue, another article was offering advice on the best ways to stay thin and the ten best bikinis that would show off their bodies, not to mention that most of the images in the magazine didn't represent normal teenagers in any way. I was stunned that many people did not feel offended by the magazine, and that it could publish such articles!

Then came my daughter's first year in middle school. It was an exciting and challenging time. She wanted to define herself by the images prevalent in the media. She was attracted to the many images around us where women and girls are portrayed in submissive photos. She was attracted to behavior that was not inclusive. It was a whole year of daily discussions about the importance of being beautiful on the inside and the outside, of the joy of being inclusive, of the wisdom in learning and expanding our knowledge, in the importance of being true to her core and who she really is, and not to allow others to define that for her.

This was not an easy year; my heart ached for her and I did not like our daily arguments, but I knew that it was my job, as mother, to guide her and not give up. It was a year of patience and perseverance for me and struggle for my daughter. I remembered the advice of a friend who told me that even though we think our kids don't hear us, they do. I learned that I cannot force her to change, but I can explain to her why I disagreed with her and keep the discussion going. By seventh grade, my daughter was a new person who defined her principles and was true to them. She excelled academically and became engaged in community service and social justice issues. She did hear me and she made me proud.

Mom Aisha

YOUR THOUGHTS

BALANCE

We've all heard the "work hard, play hard" mantra when it comes to finding balance in your life. The theory is, you should have both work and play in equal proportions to find balance. I'd have to say that this is true but would add "slow your pace," and you'll find not only balance but appreciation for the moment.

Decades ago, I was on vacation in Arizona at a wellness resort. There was an array of activities to choose from to fill my days during the week's stay. I tried Tai Chi, pottery, journaling, drumming, repelling, horseback riding, and of course, getting stretched, buffed, and polished at the spa. I wanted to sample everything to get the most out of my trip.

One morning, I had chosen to sign up for what they deemed a "Morning Cardio Hike." The hike was a fast paced, three to five-mile trek up the ridge, to a plateau, and back down again. After finishing it, I felt invigorated, awake, and somewhat accomplished.

The following day, I signed up for "Morning Reflection Hike." I met the guide and the other handful of people who didn't mind waking up just as the sun was rising. After the guide had us corralled, he began heading toward the trail – the exact same trail I had done yesterday morning. "Are you kidding me?" I thought to myself. I wouldn't have signed up for the exact same thing that I had experienced yesterday. This week was costing me a fortune, and I wanted to try different things, not have a carbon copy of the previous day.

To say that I was miffed during our ascent was an understatement. For about ten minutes I had a tirade in my mind. Why hadn't I chosen a different activity? Why was I trapped on this hike doing the same damned thing that I was doing 24 hours ago? Finally, I shook myself out of the stranglehold of my thoughts and decided to let go of the disappointment and frustration that I was experiencing. As soon as I silenced my internal pouting, something magical happened. Even though I was on the same trail as the previous day, I noticed flowers I had not seen and wildlife that seemed to appear out of nowhere. As I walked, I was pleasantly surprised by all the things that I was seeing that I hadn't seen the day before. Suddenly, I realized that what was different was our pace. Yesterday's hike had been about speed. Today's hike was about taking it slow. I had the epiphany that I was treating my life in the same manner. My MO had been about productivity and "getting things done." Although I was highly productive (by my own measuring stick), I was missing so much in life because of the backbreaking speed at which I was moving. How much had I been missing in conversations, in details, and in relationships?

The hike had been a metaphor for life. It's not just about "playing hard" that gives you balance. It's about the speed you choose on your journey. If you slow your speed, balance can also be yours.

Mom Rachel

YOUR THOUGHTS

BEAUTY

"Let beauty of what you love, be what you do."   *Rumi*
"Beauty is in the eye of the beholder."
                                        Margaret Hungerford
"Everything has its beauty, but not everyone sees it."
                                        Confucius

Life is full of beauty. You just need to stop and take notice. You will find beauty in the most mundane and extraordinary circumstances.

There is the obvious beauty of nature – sea foam oceans as far as you can see, orange and purple sunsets that take your breath away, sleeping babies that smell of fresh flowers.

There are the subtleties of beauty as in well-written prose, the perfect angle of the handcrafted chair, the aroma of fresh roasted coffee.

There is beauty in the mundane, as the child on the bus leaning against her mother, the sleeve of a favorite shirt that rests gently on your wrist. There is beauty in victory as well as loss, celebration as well as tragedy, old as well as new.

Your job in life is to notice beauty in its infinite expressions. Stop long enough to notice beauty. Beauty is everywhere, all the time, just pause long enough to take notice. In fact, your observations of beauty can improve your quality of life.

Look around and notice the beauty in whatever you see. Don't force it. Just see if you notice it in the lyric of a song or a smile from a child.

Mom Natalie

YOUR THOUGHTS

BE GENUINE

"Be who you are and say what you feel because those who mind don't matter and those who matter don't mind." Dr. Seuss

Those who matter want to know how you think and feel, so let it out. Say it. Be the one who starts the conversation, whether it be a controversial issue or just how you are feeling. Put yourself out there; you may be surprised how positively people react to your thoughts.

Mom Missy

YOUR THOUGHTS

CHALLENGES

If you are living a full life, you will have challenges.

A wise friend told me that as challenges come and go, think of yourself as a river rock. Life's challenges are the current that flows above, below, around, and through you and polishes you into the beautifully smoothed, unique stone you are destined to be. You will sometimes bump up against other rocks and stones. Some rocks will tumble miles down the river, others will stay along one river bed. But ultimately all river rocks will end up just where they were meant to be and as they were meant to be. As you will end up with the skills, knowledge, and traits that you need to become the best version of yourself.

The lesson with challenges is not to resist them but to quickly learn the lessons they are intended to teach. By integrating them into your life, you move on stronger and wiser.

Sometimes a challenge will enter into your life and you will ask, "Why me?" Well, "Why not you?"

By cultivating an attitude of acceptance and openness (and perhaps even inquisitiveness), you can face challenges without struggle and resistance. You will simply notice them, maybe even welcome them and incorporate the lesson.

Mom Natalie

Book: *From Crisis to Creativity* (Gail C. Feldman)

YOUR THOUGHTS

COMMITMENT

"Whatever you do, work at it with all your heart, working for the Lord, not for men, since you know that you will receive an inheritance from the Lord as a reward. It is the Lord Christ you are serving." Colossians 3:23-24

What is the difference between contribution and commitment? Both start with "C," but the difference between the two goes much deeper. Here is a story that I love to use to explain the difference:

A chicken and a pig were walking down the street one day when they came to a grocery store with a sign in the window that read: "Bacon and Eggs Desperately Needed." The chicken looked at the pig and said, "I'll give them the eggs if you'll give them the bacon." The pig stared at the chicken and replied, "No way!" The chicken asked, "Why not!" The pig replied, "Because for you it's just a contribution, but for me it's total commitment!"

Commitment seems to be rapidly fading in today's world. This is evident everywhere. Many people are not as committed to jobs, marriages, or even the quality of products. Even military recruitment has become more difficult, due to the commitment involved with making such a decision.

Commitment is sticking to the choice you have made, despite the obstacles. Feelings come and go; it is through commitment we carry through. True character is revealed when we have to extend ourselves unselfishly.

True commitment is about vision, growth, and continual improvement.

Mom Connie

Books: *Servant Leadership* by James C. Hunter and
Play to Win by Larry Wilson

YOUR THOUGHTS

COMMUNICATION

With the explosion of social media, communication has taken on a variety of new and different forms with texting, Instagram, Snapchat, Facebook and many more. Most of these formats encourage controlled and one-way communication, therefore limiting the essence of true interactive communication. The challenge with this indirect type of communication is that we lose what is essential and basic in effective communication – deep engagement and connection.

By definition, communication is sharing and exchanging information. It is primarily intended to be a reciprocal interaction in real time. Ideally, communication should be made up of 65% listening, 20% speaking, 9% reading, and 6% writing.

So, why do we often avoid conversations in many situations? Carrying on a conversation can be difficult even for the biggest extroverts. You are not alone in feeling awkward or shy.

Here are a few tips on how to have a meaningful conversation:

- O   Show interest and that you care by listening.
- O   Ask open-ended questions.
- O   Let the other person teach you something.
- O   Read the news.
- O   Share anecdotes; Share stories about similarities of connection.
- O   Practice FORM:

F – Family; O – Occupation; R – Recreation; M – Money.

- O   Be honest.
- O   Watch and learn from experts – talk show hosts, interviewers.
- O   Boost the other person's self-esteem.
- O   Practice with everyone, everywhere.
- O   Use the ARE:

A – Anchor (something in common); R – Reveal (share something personal); E – Encourage (invite them to share something personal).

By truly being interested in the other person and being in the moment, you will ensure a meaningful connection and deeper engagement with the other person. This is the foundation of long-term relationships.

Mom Connie

YOUR THOUGHTS

COMMUNITY

"It takes a village to raise a child." – Proverb

I am a bridge between two different, yet similar worlds. I was born and raised in Yemen and came to the US to go to college when I was seventeen years old. Yemeni traditions value the community and personal sacrifices are made for the sake of the community. American tradition on the other hand, values individualism. Both cultures value free spirits and humility. I am in a position where I can choose the values that I want to follow in my life and teach my daughter to use her own judgment in making her choices so that she can have the better of the two worlds.

When I was growing up, my parents were not the only ones I looked to for guidance and care. My uncles, aunts, grandparents, and neighbors were all part of the extensive community responsible for my wellbeing. I could go to any of them for care, and anyone had the right to admonish me if I did something wrong. As children, we could stop in any of the homes in the neighborhood for a glass of water if we were thirsty, and we often ate our meals with relatives and friends.

I learned many of the norms and values from observing how they were practiced. If there were a need in a family due to sickness, death, or even childbirth, the whole community would be there to provide care for the family. They took care of the kids, cleaned the home, cooked the meals, hosted the stream of visitors, and provided emotional support.

When I lived in Atlanta, I got a call from a friend, who sounded distressed. She explained that her two university student daughters had come home, but since she was sick in her bedroom, they left the house to get dinner and only checked on her when they came back. She was flabbergasted and could not understand what went wrong in their upbringing. She explained that when she was growing up, if her mother was sick, she knew that her priority was to take care of her mother. So why was it that her daughters, who were smart young ladies, did not do the same for her? My friend did not take into account that when her mother got sick, the whole community showed up and supported her mother. Although no one told her specifically that she needed to take care of her mother, she had learned it by observing others do it. Her daughters, in the US, in a nuclear family without the extended family, had not experienced that.

I try to emphasize the sense of community to my daughter, and I am cognizant of the values that I need to share with her as I know that she does not have the opportunity to see some of these in practice. She does travel to Yemen and Lebanon for short periods and gets a chance to be part of a larger community. Her favorite place is the village Lasa in Lebanon, where every home is welcoming and people treat her like she is one of the family.

Mom Aisha

YOUR THOUGHTS

COMPASSION

In the Quran, God is referred to as merciful and compassionate 114 times.

Compassion plays an important role in parenting and all that we do. It is compassion that allows parents to care for and love their children. It also is the pillar that we rely on especially during difficult interactions. It is an important trait to cultivate and instill in ourselves and others.

I had a friend who was told that she had a few months to live. She was the most positive person I have ever met. She took the news in stride following an Arabic proverb: "Do for this life as if you will live forever and do for the afterlife as if you will die tomorrow." She often needed to be admitted to the hospital. She travelled when she could and bought another home on the beach in Florida. One thing that we both knew brought her joy was interacting with my strong willed two-year-old daughter. When she had hard days, if she was at home, I would take my daughter to spend some time with her, and she would always have some activity for the two of them. If she was at the hospital, I would take my daughter to the hospital every day before I dropped her off at the daycare center until a nurse once stopped us, because children were not allowed in the unit.

In one of her visits to her Florida home, I called to talk to her and learned that she was not doing well. My husband and I decided to travel to see her with our daughter to cheer her up. When we got there, we found that she had collected real estate information to persuade us to purchase a second home in Florida. We went to see a few homes on our last day, and we purchased one that same day, not far from where she lived. My friend passed away a few years after the doctors told her she had a few months to live. We still own the home in Florida, and we have some of our best family memories there. When I walk on

the beach, I find myself talking to her and feel that she is smiling as she sees my daughter grow to be an independent, compassionate young woman.

Mom Aisha

YOUR THOUGHTS

COMPLETION

"Great is the art of beginning, but greater is the art of ending." Henry Wadsworth Longfellow

Ever find yourself holding onto something, because you didn't want to be seen as a quitter, or you wanted to keep the peace, or you wanted to please somebody?

Maybe you're stuck in a job or with a manager who squashed your creativity, undermined your authority, or belittled you?

Maybe it has nothing to do with work, but is a friendship you've kept that is stress-inducing. Or a marriage that is emotionally hurtful, or maybe even physically hurtful, but you're too scared to let go? Or how about that family member who drains you, but you keep going back for more. Can anybody relate?

These are what Henry Cloud calls necessary endings, and it's the title of a book I just finished reading. Actually just finished listening to. What would we do without Audible? If you haven't been exposed to Audible yet, it's time. Audible is a great way to take advantage of moments in the car or chores around the house. Okay, back to the topic. These necessary endings aren't about quitting; they're about recognizing when hope is lost for things to get better and making a necessary and intentional plan to bring something, whether a relationship, job, or behavior to an end.

This has been a huge shift in my "don't be a quitter" mindset. According to Cloud, "Without the ability to end things, people stay stuck, never becoming who they are meant to be, never accomplishing all that their talents and abilities should afford them." I had never looked at endings that way. I tended to see them as failure or quitting versus something that could be holding me back.

If you're like this too, and stuck thinking you have to stick things out, consider shifting your thinking and look at it through a different lens. Everything has an end just like everything has a beginning. Cloud says that when we look at life, we can see this play out everywhere; our kids must stop crawling in order to walk. They must also stop relying on us in order to leave the nest and build their own adult lives. We stop watering the lawn in the fall to allow it to go dormant for the winter season. Endings. They're everywhere.

Cloud asks, "...are there situations in business or in life where you are trying to birth things that should be dying? Trying to heal something that should be killed off? Laughing at something that you should be weeping about? Embracing something (or someone) you should shun? Searching for an answer for something when it is time to give up? Continuing to try to love something or someone when it is time to talk about what you hate?"

What necessary endings do you have to close in your life? Remember, it's not about quitting; it's about making a start to something better. Think of it like pruning. "Pruning is strategic. It is directional and forward-looking. It is intentional toward a vision, desires, and objectives that have been clearly defined and are measurable." Henry Cloud

Book: *Necessary Endings: The Employees, Businesses, and Relationships That All of Us Have to Give Up in Order to Move Forward* by Henry Cloud

Mom Jenny

YOUR THOUGHTS

CREATIVITY

"Creativity is just connecting things. When you ask creative people how they did something, they feel a little guilty, because they didn't really do it, they just saw something. It seemed obvious to them after a while." – Steve Jobs

Creativity and innovative problem solving are highly sought and often hard-to-find skills. However, over the years, I have realized that we can all be creative. The first step is to embrace not knowing all the answers, then be willing to think outside your own comfort zone. One tool that I have found extremely helpful in my life, and I have shared to help countless others is SCAMPER:

S = Substitute
C = Combine
A = Adapt
M = Magnify
P = Put to Other Uses
E = Eliminate (or Minify)
R = Rearrange (or Reverse)

SCAMPER is an easy, yet powerful method you can use to encourage creativity and help problem solve almost any challenge. In essence, SCAMPER is a general-purpose checklist with idea-spurring questions based on the premise that everything new is a modification of something that already exists. It was created by Bob Eberle in the early 70s, and it has stood the test of time.

Each letter in the acronym represents a different way you can view the challenge. Asking questions using SCAMPER forces you to think differently about your problem and eventually come up with innovative solutions.

For example, if your challenge is, "How can I increase sales in my business?" Here are a few questions you could ask:

Substitute: "What can I substitute in my selling process?"

Combine: "How can I combine selling with other activities?"

Adapt: "What can I adapt or copy from someone else's selling process?"

Magnify: "What can I magnify or put more emphasis on when selling?"

Put to Other Uses: "How can I put my selling to other uses?"

Eliminate: "What can I eliminate or simplify in my selling process?"

Rearrange: "How can I change, reorder, or reverse the way I sell?"

As Albert Einstein so aptly stated: *"We cannot solve our problems with the same thinking we used when we created them."*

Mom Connie

YOUR THOUGHTS

DECISION MAKING

Start now! Making decisions that are clear and firm in your beliefs and God's will prepare you for a journey of confidence, growth, and success.

But how do we know that our decisions are "right?" How do we gain confidence to move forward? Well, this is where it begins. You have been given a great mind and the ability to discern what is right and wrong – we call that free agency. Morals, religious background, life experiences, societal norms, watching as others walk their journey, listening and gaining insights – all help you, but ultimately YOU are responsible and accountable for your choices.

A very simple and clear way to learn how to "decide" begins by understanding that getting to a decision is not complex or layered in drama. You either feel peaceful or confused about the issue or problem you face. The scriptures teach us that we will, "....feel a burning in the bosom...or a stupor of thought (confusion)."

So, in learning how to make a choice:
     First: Identify the issue.
     Second: Ponder the options (pros and cons).
     Third: Choose one and put it to prayer for confirmation. For i.e., Dear Heavenly Father, I have chosen to_____ because of _____ (these reasons), please confirm if this is Thy will.

If you are to act on the decision you will clearly know in your head and heart that it is right, or have a peaceful feeling (burning in the bosom). If it is not God's will at the time, you will undoubtedly feel confused, filled with drama, and not be at peace. What takes time to learn are *trust and faith*. Take the confirmation of your decision and act upon it. If your head is filled with fear, contempt, lack of faith, or a whole slew of emotions, it will be very difficult to hear the Holy Spirit confirm God's will.

So, remember to be "still" and not let the adversary (Satan) bombard you with a ton of emotions circling through your head that keep you from the clear path of hearing. God will not fail you! P.S. Don't forget to thank Him.

Mom Jay

YOUR THOUGHTS

ENDURANCE

Definition: Endurance is the fact or power of enduring an unpleasant or difficult process or situation without giving way:

Endurance, perhaps one of the most difficult words in the English language. Has life been unpleasant and/or difficult? I would answer yes! Sometimes daily. That said, I am so thankful I do not have to create endurance on my own or of my own volition. I find it quite a relief to admit, on my own, I do not have the endurance required for the unpleasant or difficult processes and situations in my life.

My relationship with God is my key to experiencing endurance. God is more powerful than I am and therefore my source of endurance. In the Bible, Philippians 4:13 says, "*I can do all things through Him who strengthens me.*" God is my power and when I am tempted to give way to stress, fear, worry, etc. I am encouraged to know and experience endurance from Him.

Be encouraged, He is able to give you all the endurance you need!

Mom Gina

Book: *The Holy Bible*

YOUR THOUGHTS

FAITH

"Faith is taking the first step even when you don't see the whole staircase." Martin Luther King, Jr.

A universal saying captures the trust in God people of faith have: "God works in mysterious ways." We don't necessarily understand logically why things happen the way they do, but we trust God with our hearts that He has a good reason for why. We believe that God has the best plans for us, and sometimes, what seems to be a hardship, is a path to something better. We may hate something and in it is the best for us. Faith comes from the heart and for those who believe in God, it is the source of strength that enables them to withstand the most challenging of circumstances.

When I was 30 years of age, I experienced the most challenging hardship in my life; every moment of the day was painful. It felt that committing suicide would be less painful than enduring the pain I was feeling. The only reason I endured was because in my faith, suicide is not forgiven by God. My faith saved me during my darkest hours. I prayed constantly, "God, I don't ask that you change my situation, but I do pray that you give me the strength to endure." I am grateful now that I had my faith to help me pass through that year in my life.

Since then, like every human being, I have experienced other challenges, but I have been less impacted; that year strengthened my resolve and made me a stronger person. I figured that if I was delivered from that experience and had many blessings in my life, then I could trust that God would help me overcome my problems and strengthen my resolve.

When my daughter was younger she came home one day and told me that she was an atheist. I did not react negatively since I knew that would not help. After a few discussions, I told her that I would like for her to learn about faith before she rejected it. My point was, you couldn't reject something because you don't know enough about it. I shared with her how faith allowed me to be present with her and to enjoy the blessing of being her mother. I told her how faith was my anchor that made sure that I did not drift in the waters of life aimlessly. I told her that I wanted faith to be there for her when she felt that no one else was with her, as God would always be with her.

A dear Presbyterian minister once asked me when I knew that God was present; I told him that God was always present, but we get too distracted in our daily lives to recognize that. That reminded me of writings by Tagore, an Indian philosopher: "I woke up in the morning with a letter from God next to my bed. I did not have to open it as the wind, the leaves on the trees, and the sound of water were reciting the words in my letter."

Mom Aisha

Book: *The Holy Bible* and *Quran*

YOUR THOUGHTS

FITTING IN

Throughout life we often struggle to fit in and find our place. We look to others for affirmations and value. We compare, judge, and ridicule ourselves for body type, looks, education, career, money, status, and the like.

I recently purchased seven ceramic birds that fit in the palm of the hand. Each has a unique color; each has a unique stance. But one bird has a beak different from the rest. As I sit with my seven grandchildren, we discuss the beauty of each bird and the uniqueness of the beak on one. I ask, "Which one are you?" They find the one that represents them and identify the reasons why. I talk about each one being a unique bird and the value of gifts and talents unlike the rest.

We discuss what it is to be unique and "different." They hear how wonderful it is to stand differently and sometimes alone without anyone noticing. They learn the value of inclusion and cooperation. They learn about getting beyond looking alike, acting alike, and other similarities – how special it is that the birds fly on their own and travel high in the sky.

Lately, as the older grandkids visit the ceramic birds, a new discussion has surfaced: "Grandma, I was the unique bird today, because I helped my teacher." I have heard so many precious reasons why being "different" has helped them to value themselves. We too, need to remember to fly high with our unique ways. Value who you are and instead of wondering why you don't fit in, find the reason why it's so spectacular that you are who you were made to be.

Mom Jay

YOUR THOUGHTS

FORGIVENESS

Some of the hardest work in your life will center around forgiveness. The quick response of, "I'm sorry," or "I forgive you," takes you to the depth of your soul to seek peace from an injury.

It is true that forgiveness saves the soul of an individual. Harboring anger, hate, and lack of peace destroys who you are. When you are in the depth of despair call out for God's arms to surround you and then become "still." Quiet your anguish; quiet your pain until you are safe to proceed. What will happen in your stillness is a miracle and gift from the Holy Spirit, who will enter and guide you to a peace and strength you cannot imagine. The healing that comes, transforms you from being a broken soul to spiritual completeness. It is amazing.

This is a process that requires vigilance and time. God does not hurry but rather walks us gently through each layer. He rebuilds us to be more complete and better. He helps us face what is ours and rest what is another's. Heed the wisdom that you hear from the Holy Spirit and get within your soul to do the work. All other facades and pretenses are false and will not build you but rather block the potential you have been given.

No one deserves a space in your life to ruin it. No one deserves center stage for too long. This is your dance and along with God your performance will be amazing.

Mom Jay

Books: *The Holy Bible* and *Jacob the Baker*
by Noah benShea

YOUR THOUGHTS

FRIENDSHIP

It is said that if you can count on one hand the number of "real" friends in your life than you are lucky indeed.

What is friendship?

A true friend is loyal, kind, trustworthy, sees the very best in you, walks with you through the storms, gives you grace for your faults, laughs with you, and cries when you cry.

Do you act like the friend you want to have?

What do your friends say about the kind of friend you are to them?

A true friend knows your weaknesses but shows you your strengths; feels your fears but fortifies your faith; sees your anxieties but frees your spirit; recognizes your disabilities but emphasizes your possibilities. W.A. Ward

Mom Connie

YOUR THOUGHTS

GOODNESS

"Good is something you do, not something you talk about. Some medals are pinned to your soul, not to your jacket. You must do good, but must not talk about it. If you talk about it you're taking advantage of others' misfortunes for your gain."
Gino Bartali

To understand this quote, it is important to learn who Gino Bartali was. He was a cyclist that won the Giro D'Italia twice and the Tour de France once. During WWII, he joined a secret network and became a courier hiding photographs and counterfeit identity papers inside the frame of his bicycle to help save endangered people. He never wanted to be recognized for his efforts. He spent the rest of his life quietly and never boasted about the risks or danger he endured to help others. While others wanted to praise him for his bravery, he preferred not to be recognized for his good deeds.

With social media and news spreading far and wide almost instantly, it is common to see people receiving accolades for helping others, making donations, and helping communities in need. For some, the need for praise and adoration is their ulterior motive for the good deed. It becomes more about them and not the deed itself. It also puts a spotlight on those who are hurting, which may contribute to their hurt if they are private in nature, prideful, or have a hard time receiving assistance. It is not easy for some people to ask for help. If you are going to do something good for someone else, consider doing it anonymously or quietly. Do you need everyone to know what you have done? Can you take pride in knowing you helped someone without fanfare? Take joy in knowing you helped. Be humble. Be kind.

Mom Sharin

YOUR THOUGHTS

GRATITUDE

"Gratitude is not only the greatest of virtues, but the parent of all others." Marcus Tullius Cicero

"Be thankful for what you have; you'll end up having more. If you concentrate on what you don't have, you will never, ever have enough." Oprah Winfrey

Gratitude can be practiced. When you stop, take notice and give thanks for everything – a beautiful sunrise, a great meal, a good friend – the practice of gratitude can become a habit. Once this habit is established, it will enhance your life beyond measure. It is fine to be grateful for what the world calls good fortune – good grades, money, and championships – there is nothing wrong with these things coming your way. But the kind of gratitude that will fill your soul is the gratitude for the intangibles in life, like a kind word, a gentle smile, and the beauty of nature.

Practice gratitude each day. Just as you would go to the gym to work out your body, work out your gratitude muscle. Watch it grow and fill your life with wonder.

Mom Natalie

Book: *Attitudes of Gratitude* by M. J. Ryan

YOUR THOUGHTS

GRIT

"Grit is that 'extra something' that separates the most successful people from the rest. It's the passion, perseverance, and stamina that we must channel in order to stick with our dreams until they become a reality." Travis Bradberry

Grit is more important than talent. This was proven in the late 1960's by Stanford psychologist Walter Mischel in the now-iconic *Marshmallow Test*. This experiment analyzed the ability of four-year-olds to demonstrate "delayed gratification." Look it up. Fascinating.

Self-control is important in determining your ability to follow through on certain difficult tasks or challenges. However, Angela Duckworth, Harvard research, determined the most important factor in predicting success and high-challenge achievement is "grit."

Grit is defined as "the perseverance and passion for a long-term goal." Tenacity is at the heart of every outstanding achievement. The ability not to look for a change or be distracted by novelty is critical. The ability not to abandon tasks in the face of obstacles or challenges is essential. "True grit" is the foundation of remarkable achievement.

Mom Connie

Book: *Don't Eat the Marshmallow... Yet!*
by Joachim de Posada

YOUR THOUGHTS

HAPPINESS

Happiness is a choice.

"Most people are about as happy as they make up their minds to be." – *Abraham Lincoln*

Naturally, we all want to be happy. However, there are times in life when feeling happy can be rather difficult. Trying to find an inner joy may feel like a true struggle. But it's important to remember that whatever you are going through, it's never too late to make happiness your **choice.**

Happiness can be defined as God's blessing inside of you, no matter what happens outside of you. By trusting in God, we will be comforted by Him and can overcome the barriers that cause us to be unhappy.

Author Joshua Becker wrote about "12 Intentional Actions to Choose Happiness Today":

1. **Count your blessings**. Focus on the positive rather than the negative. Express gratitude to those around you. This will not only make you happy, but others as well.

2. **Smile!** By doing so you, your brain releases endorphins responsible for making us feel happy and lowering stress levels.

3. **Speak daily affirmation into your life.** These are positive personal statements of truth. Don't be afraid to say you are confident. You are strong. You are smart. You are beautiful. You are important.

4. **Wake up on your terms.** Don't be rushed. Control your morning routine in order to start your day in a meaningful way.

5. **Hold back a complaint.** Choose to keep criticism or dissatisfaction to yourself in a difficult situation. Stay humble and kind. You may find you've diffused an unhappy environment.

6. **Practice one life-improving discipline.** Perform one act of self-discipline each day that will provide a positive step toward personal growth.

7. **Use your strengths.** Embrace your strengths and utilize your natural talents.

8. **Accomplish one important task.** Choose something important to be accomplished, take control, and celebrate your achievement.

9. **Eat a healthy meal/snack.** Caring for our physical well-being can have a significant benefit for our emotional health.

10. **Treat others well.** "Do unto others as you would have them do unto you." Respecting others and being kind benefits not only the receiver but brings about self-satisfaction.

11. **Meditate.** Take a break and clear your mind. Learning to meditate can connect you spiritually in order to achieve improved happiness.

12. **Search for benefit in your pain.** Life is difficult! Choose to find the meaning of your pain and search for benefits that can be found. Let go of the things that make you sad.

Most importantly, as you choose happiness, be reminded of Psalm 37:4, "Seek your happiness in the Lord, and he will give you your heart's desire."

Mom Mary Kay

Book: *The More of Less: Finding the Life You Want Under Everything You Own* by Joshua Becker

YOUR THOUGHTS

HOPE

"Don't lose hope nor be sad." Quran 3:139

Life is full of challenges and hope is the key to overcoming those challenges. As the war in Yemen wages for over 1000 days with a blockade that limits basic essential goods entry into Yemen, my heart aches for the people. My daughter is distraught by this and at times cries and asks me why I don't show more sorrow or anguish? She asks if I am hiding my sad emotions from her. I explain that my heart is in constant pain, but that hope is the key to staying positive and knowing that this is only a phase that will pass, no matter the length of the phase.

Hope is the window that allows us to see beyond the heartache. It helps us see the light at the end of the tunnel. It motivates us to act to make the change we desire happen. This is how people survive the most challenging ordeals they face, whether that is in a war zone, a natural disaster, a sickness, or a personal setback.

In response to the dire situation in Yemen, I started raising funds to support those in need. Within six months, I received more donations than I ever anticipated, leading me to establish a foundation. I also started speaking in public forms about the situation in Yemen and the US role in the war, and working with other national and local groups interested in ending the war in Yemen. These efforts paid off with more people reaching out to our politicians in Washington D.C., asking that the US end its support for the war.

My daughter followed suit. She made a presentation to her class about the dire situation in Yemen, prompting her classmates to support several activities in their school to support the relief efforts in Yemen. They organized a bake sale, sold Yemeni jewelry, and organized two presentations at the school. Others asked if they could support the new foundation by designing the logo for a class project. All these efforts showcased how hardships can bring people together to alleviate the suffering of people they have not met.

I talk to my family and friends in Yemen, and they try to comfort me by telling me that all is well. They say that this is the birth of a new Yemen, one that will be inclusive and without much foreign influence. They quote the Quran: "Surely, with every hardship, there is relief. Verily, with hardship, there is relief." 94:5-6. They remind me that the relief is present with every hardship, not after it! Indeed, this is the ultimate hope in God's mercy that comes from faith.

Mom Aisha

Books: *The Holy Bible* and *Quran*

YOUR THOUGHTS

HUMOR

"Always laugh when you can. It is cheap medicine." Lord Byron

Turn on the nightly news or read about the tragic events on your scrolling CNN feed, and you will be bombarded with negativity. It is easy to fall prey to the content that is broadcasted. If you are inundated only by stories, which like quicksand, can slowly bury you, it's so important to surround yourself with positive, optimistic people who can make you laugh. Better yet, be one of those people who can make someone grin from ear to ear or cry so hard from laughing that they are literally rolling on the floor. (How do you think ROTFL came to be?)

Sure, there is a time and place for everything, but laughter is the best pick-me-up. Not only does it help relieve stressful situations, but it has the power to transform a scowling, intimidating man into a teddy bear.

The ability to make someone laugh is a special talent. So, if you happen to be blessed with the gift to make others laugh, by all means use it!

I can't tell you how many kids I went to school with who were the proverbial "class clowns," who are now successful CEOs or influence makers. If you want a simple, cost-free way to make a high impact on somebody, use humor. It breaks down barriers, lowers anxiety, and is just downright effective in lightening your mood.

Mom Rachel

YOUR THOUGHTS

IDENTITY

What is your brand? Like me, some of the moms in this book spent their careers marketing brands for Fortune 500 companies. We were the ones deciding what the public image was for the product or service that ultimately drove sales. Although I did that successfully for different companies throughout my career, it wasn't until recently that someone asked me, "What is your brand?" I looked at the person asking and had her repeat the question. After a few minutes of pondering, I told her that I'd have to give it more thought. I could rattle off the attributes of dozens of products for which I had created brand identities, but when it came to my own brand, I seemed to be at a loss.

After much reflection, I decided that I want my personal brand to be: "I am a creative communicator who is cause-oriented." How did I come up with that? Well, first off, I chose three C's because it was easy to remember! Secondly, I know that I like to write, speak, and inspire people, so that's where the first of the two attributes came from. The last characteristic is because I have spent a great deal of time in the nonprofit world and continue to support causes that are close to my heart. I did have "compassionate" as a close fourth, but following my own rules to confine it to the big three, I reasoned that compassion could fall under my umbrella of cause-oriented.

My advice is simple: don't wait five decades to know YOUR "brand. Once you define the top three traits that you wish to be known for, they help direct your choice of words, actions, and deeds. Your brand should be your divining rod that points you in the right direction each day. Whatever your three words are, (of course there are hundreds of characteristics that could be used to describe you, but I'm asking you to select your top three) you want to walk that way, talk that way, think that way, behave that way, dream that way! You get the picture. Your brand should be so clear and evident that when others are asked about you, you hear those three traits rattled back to you.

"Wow, Janine is undaunted!"

"Sarah, she is so loyal!"

"Connie is inspiring!"

Don't just create brands for companies, be your own CMO (Chief Marketing Officer). Once you do, your choices in life become so easy, because all you need to do is ask yourself, "Does it align with my brand?" If you want to be perceived as kind and selfless, do you help friends when they are moving or when they need a shoulder to cry on? Do you let others cut in front of you in traffic? Do you write thank you notes or letters of accommodation for people who serve you during the day? Your brand may change during different phases of your life. However, your mission is to always realign with your stated brand. Once you have done this, your compass for life is always by your side!

Mom Rachel

YOUR THOUGHTS

INDEPENDENCE

"They who can give up essential liberty to obtain a little temporary safety deserve neither liberty nor safety." Benjamin Franklin

We all want to be independent, especially during adolescence. Independence comes with a price, and those who are willing to make sacrifices to maintain their independence succeed in attaining their objective.

Women traditionally depended on their husbands or male family members for support. That is partly due to the responsibilities placed on women for taking care of the home and children. As more women started to join the work force, many continued to be the main caretaker for the family. That created a dilemma, and many women had to make hard choices between advancing their careers by putting in the unacceptably long work hours, staying at home, or forfeiting promotions to allow time for the family.

Many of us want the approval of those around us, especially our loved ones. Sometimes we yield to the expectations and opinions of other people in making our decisions. However, in doing so, it is our lives that are affected. When I met my husband, my parents were not happy as they had hoped that I would marry someone from Yemen. After six years of negotiations, I failed to convince them. I had to decide, marry the person I loved and leave my family, or stay with my family and leave him. In the context of my family having done everything for me, including paying for all my educational costs in the US from undergraduate to graduate studies, and being from Yemen, where an individual sacrifices for the community, this was the most difficult decision I had made in my life. Ultimately, I refused the dichotomy and chose both.

I have a strong-willed daughter who has a strong streak of independence. I learned early on to let her make her own decisions, even when I did not think they were the best. As a youngster, she refused to wear heavy clothing during the winter; I let her be, knowing that if she felt cold, then she would let me know. However, I got many angry looks from people when we were in public; the assumption was that I was a negligent mother. I learned to discuss why I wanted her to do certain things and gave her options and let her make the final decision. That was not an easy task as I did not always have the time or energy to do this; my solace was that this would help her in the long run as she went out into the world where women still are not treated fairly.

Learning to make independent decisions, especially in matters that are important in ones' life, is essential to our happiness. Although we may seek advice from others in making decisions, in the end it is our responsibility to synthesize the advice and to make decisions that fit with our lives, as no one knows our hearts like us.

Mom Aisha

YOUR THOUGHTS

INSTINCT

Trust your gut instinct.

Listen to that nagging voice or feeling telling you something is not right. If you feel that someone, something, or a situation is off, pay attention. Your body is telling you something is wrong and warning you to protect yourself. Leave the situation you are presently in. Don't participate in an activity that you don't feel good about. Steer clear of that person that is giving you bad vibes. You are not going crazy or being paranoid.

Your body is an incredible, complex work of art. It has the ability to pick up on negative vibrations and can trigger a queasy feeling right in the pit of your stomach. Don't ignore it. Listen to it and protect yourself. You may never know what consequence may have occurred if you didn't listen to your gut instinct. That is okay. There is a reason that this protection was built into our systems.

Trust it. Listen to it. Let it guide and protect you.

Mom Sharin

YOUR THOUGHTS

INTUITION

"The only real valuable thing is intuition." - Albert Einstein

A dear friend, who was a Presbyterian minister, once gave me a book titled, "The God Who Speaks." After reading the book, I was able to understand what we may call our "sixth sense" or intuition. Many of us suppress our initial feelings or reactions, because they don't seem logical.

In our fast-moving world, we can have thousands of virtual friends, spend hours interacting with people we have never met, and constantly stream videos on every possible subject. This lack of human interaction that we increasingly face makes it even more important to develop a keen sense of intuition.

I had an experience with intuition when my daughter, who started daycare at three years of age, made a comment about her daycare teacher, who was considered the best. My daughter came home after a week in the class and said that she did not want to be in the teacher's class, but she could not articulate why. As a parent, I was concerned and struggled with making sense of her comments versus the good reputation of the teacher. However, I certainly did not want to dismiss my daughter's comments and I wanted to encourage her always to express her concerns freely and bring them to my attention. It never occurred to me that her feelings were childish or had no foundation. I tried to understand the reasons for what sounded like a "gut feeling" my daughter shared with me. I decided that I would trust her feelings, and I went to the daycare and requested that my daughter be moved to another room. I was told that the daycare policy did not allow moving children between rooms and that her room had the best teacher, but I insisted. She was moved, and within the next year, more children and parents spoke up, and the teacher had to leave the daycare. This experience reinforced my resolve to trust my daughter's intuition, even though at times I couldn't understand the reason for her feelings. I always tell her to trust her feelings.

It is important to distinguish between biases we may have about other people that may lead us to feel uneasy around them and true intuition that can't be explained by our prejudices and biases. One thing I know for sure, intuition, sixth sense, or the voice of God is there to protect us and not to harm anyone.

Mom Aisha

Book: *The God Who Speaks* by Ben Campbell Johnston

YOUR THOUGHTS

JOY

"The Joy of the Lord is my strength." Nehemiah 8:10

If I had one word to share with my daughter, it would be JOY. One of the precious things in life is to experience joy every day, in every situation of our lives. How do you do this? Joy can be simply stated, but at times a hard lesson to learn, practice, and refine.

J = Joy
O = Others
Y = Yourself

In fact, you can sing it to the tune of Jingle Bells: "J-O-Y, J-O-Y, this is what it means: Jesus first, yourself last, and others in between."

With us accepting Jesus into our hearts, we know He loves us unconditionally. Assisting others with service, kindness, and even sweet thoughts will bring unexplainable JOY into our hearts and our minds.

Put yourself last because we understand we are a blessing and loved unconditionally by Jesus. If we depend on Jesus as our best friend, we will have boundless energy to serve and to love life. For even more joy, we shouldn't take ourselves too seriously; we should laugh at our mistakes and misfortunes! We had the courage and strength of the Lord to laugh about my daughter's bald head while fighting cancer.

Mom Joyce

YOUR THOUGHTS

KINDNESS

I love this story about making a difference and extending kindness.

"While walking along a beach, an elderly gentleman saw someone in the distance leaning down, picking something up, and throwing it into the ocean.

As he got closer, he noticed that the figure was that of a young man, picking up starfish one by one and tossing each one gently back into the water.

The gentleman came closer still and called out, "Good morning! May I ask what it is that you are doing?"

The young man paused, looked up, and replied, "Throwing starfish into the ocean."

The old man smiled, and said, "I must ask, then, why are you throwing starfish into the ocean?"

To this the young man replied, "The sun is up and the tide is going out. If I don't throw them in, they'll die."

Upon hearing this, the elderly observer commented, "But, young man, do you not realize that there are miles and miles of beach, and there are starfish all along every mile? You can't possibly make a difference!"

*The young man listened politely. Then he bent down, picked up another starfish, threw it the back into the ocean past the breaking waves and said, **"It made a difference for that one."***
Author Unknown

Kindness is about how we act and being kind is simple. It's giving attention, appreciation, and encouragement.

Let's break it down further.

Attention –

The greatest opportunity to pay attention to people is by "active listening." If you listen selectively, you make judgments with partial information. Active listening requires discipline to silence your own internal conversation. It requires a sacrifice to extend ourselves. It is attempting to see things as the speaker sees them and feel the things the speaker feels. Identification with the speaker is empathy and requires effort. Empathy is being fully present – physically, emotionally, and mentally. Communication is 65% listening. Listening or not sends conscious and unconscious messages. You are willing to set aside all distractions; it says you care; it tells the person they are important and valued. Just listening and sharing the problem with the other person immediately eases their burden. There is a cathartic effect in being listened to and being allowed to express feelings with another. People want attention to what they say, even more than achieving. Paying attention is a legitimate need. Primary works of love are paying attention to people and listening.

Appreciation –

At the core of human personality is the need to be appreciated. In the military, soldiers have said that they won't sell their lives, but they would give them for a medal. Everyone has a billboard: on the front it says, "Appreciate Me," and on the back it says, "Make Me Feel Important."

"Be kind to others. How far you go in life depends on your being tender with the young, compassionate with the aged, sympathetic with the striving, tolerant of the weak and the strong. Because someday in your life, you will have been all of these." George Washington Carver

Encouragement –

You often find exactly what you are looking for in life. Praise is a legitimate need and essential in healthy relationships.

To truly encourage others you must be sincere and specific. This is a gift that multiplies substantially and changes lives.

So why is being kind so hard sometimes when it seems so simple? In my experience, there are two primary reasons. One, we are not in the moment and distracted by our own agenda. Two, we feel vulnerable in extending beyond ourselves for the benefit of another.

By making kindness a principle, we connect with others in a meaningful and purposeful way that can change the world.

Mom Connie

YOUR THOUGHTS

LEADERSHIP

True leadership is putting those you lead **first**. Good leaders inspire; great leaders serve.

What is leadership? By definition, leadership is the ability to **engage** people to work **purposefully** toward a common **goal** that benefits the **greater good**.

At the foundation of any relationship and at the heart of leadership is **trust**. People follow a leader because of who they are – their **character**. Successful leaders are not only competent in their chosen endeavor but also have a character that others aspire to.

Some characteristics of a good leader include:

- Honest	- Role Model
- Respectful	- Appreciative
- Caring	- Accountable
- Listens	- Encouraging
- Committed	- Enthusiastic

We are not born with these qualities; they are learned by choice. Leadership begins with **WILL**, which is our ability to *choose our behavior* by aligning intentions with actions. With a strong will, we can choose to **LOVE**, the verb, which is identifying and meeting legitimate needs of those we lead.

One of the world's most successful leaders, Vince Lombardi, said it best:

"I don't necessarily have to like my players and associates, but as their leader I must love them. Love is loyalty, love is

teamwork, and love respects the dignity of the individual. This is the strength of any organization."

What does a leader do? A leader must excel at three critical objectives.

ENVISION the FUTURE: Recognize trends, define the Team's purpose, and set future direction.

ENABLE the TEAM: Break down barriers and align resources to accomplish the Team's goals.

EMPOWER the INDIVIDUAL: Hold yourself and the Team accountable to reach each person's full potential.

The best leader of all time is Jesus. For over 2000 years across two billion Christians, Jesus changed the world without exercising power or fear. Jesus changed the world by **serving** others.

In love and in leadership, it is not about what you get but what you **give**, not about how you feel but how you **behave**. Lead from the back.

Mom Connie

Book: *Servant Leadership* by James C. Hunter

YOUR THOUGHTS

LET GO

Forgiveness is the act of letting go, giving up resentment when wronged. People aren't perfect and sometimes they let you down. To forgive is not to forget, but to still love and to move beyond. Forgiveness is more for you than others.

But resentment, anger, and hate – these destroy the human personality, leading to bitterness and unhappiness. Holding a grudge will hurt only you.

"The fist starves the hand." Jacob the Baker

Forgiving is setting yourself free from the pain someone has caused you. Forgiveness is true freedom, peace from an injury.

Mom Connie

Book: *The Road Less Traveled* by Morgan Scott Peck

YOUR THOUGHTS

LISTENING

"We have two ears and one mouth so that we can listen twice as much as we speak." Epictetus

The greatest opportunity to pay attention to people is by "active listening." If you listen selectively, you may make judgments with partial information. Active listening requires discipline to silence your own internal conversation. It requires sacrifice, to extend ourselves. It is attempting to see things as the speaker sees them and feel things as the speaker feels. Identification with the speaker is empathy and requires effort.

Listening or not sends conscious and unconscious messages. You are willing to set aside all distractions; it says you care; it tells the person they are important and valued. Just listening and sharing the problem with the other person immediately eases their burden. There is a cathartic effect in being listened to and being allowed to express feelings to another. People want attention paid to what they say, even more than achievement. Paying attention is a legitimate need. A primary work of love is paying attention to people (listening).

To learn more – listen. Listening is for understanding…not simply responding.

"Seek first to understand, then be understood." Stephen Covey

Mom Connie

Book: *Seven Habits of Highly Successful People*
by Stephen Covey

YOUR THOUGHTS

LOVE

"Explanation by words makes most things clear, but love unexplained is clearer." Persian poet, Rumi

My daughter asks me who I love most. I am never able to answer her question, because love has many forms. I tell her that there are many kinds of love: there is love for God, love for parents, love for her, love for siblings, husband, friends, country, objects, etc. Each of the above groups evokes an emotion that is different from the others, and those emotions are not comparable nor can they be put on a scale. Even the intensity of the emotions for the same person may vary depending on time and circumstance.

In Arabic, there are fifty words for love. For example, "worship" is a word of love that describes our love for God. Sufis in Islam proclaim their love for God and devote their art, including music and dance, to that. People who worship God because they love God tend to be more compassionate toward others, as this kind of love makes the heart tender. Some people may tell their loved ones, "I worship you," to express their love. Other words include love that implies friendliness, mercy, and one that describes a form of romantic love: "crazy in love."

Love is like a rainbow with all the vibrant colors and shades in between; it brightens our lives and lifts our spirits. It warms our hearts and makes us compassionate. It is the glue that holds relationships together whether between two people, in a home, community, or country. It induces all forms of emotions and sometimes even opposing ones from happy to sad. In 6th century BC, the Chinese General San Tzu, in his book "Art of War," writes that the secret to the success of a ruler is not military might, but rather, his love for his people.

True love requires sacrifices, whether it is parents sacrificing for their children, soldiers for their country or those who volunteer for various causes. These sacrifices are given willingly and without any hesitation or regret. The story of a mother's love comes to mind; she was willing to give up her son rather than cause him harm. Two women go to King Solomon each claiming to be the mother. King Solomon suggested splitting the baby into two parts and each of the women would get half. The true mother cried, proclaiming that she was not the mother.

I hope that we continue to define love with all the forms that it encompasses and not limit it to romantic love or subject it to a scale, because love should not be contained; it should be free to define itself based on the moment and situation.

Mom Aisha

Books: *The Holy Bible* and *Quran*

YOUR THOUGHTS

ORIGINALITY

You are a big thumbprint.

You can spend a tremendous amount of wasted time having anxiety and creating needless stress by trying to fit in.
"Do I have the right clothes?"
"Do I drive a nice car?"
"Do I hang out with the cool kids?"
"Am I pretty enough?"
"Am I smart enough" Am I skinny enough?"
.....Enough!

This is just a small sample of the litany of questions we torture ourselves with daily. Irony is that nobody else is like you. The fact that you are unique is what makes you special. Nobody else can be you! That is your true gift.

If you spend your time on the hamster wheel, endlessly chasing something elusive, you're just going to find yourself exhausted. Own who you are. The sooner you realize that you have certain qualities that nobody else possesses, the sooner you will see the beauty that is you.

Mom Rachel

YOUR THOUGHTS

PERSONAL INVENTORY

I have heard it said that, "contention is always selfishness." In our closest relationships, it is often difficult to do personal inventory and identify our own selfishness. It is easy to project our pain onto someone else and blame him or her. It is hard to take responsibility for our inadequacies. Who wants to be "wrong"? Who wants to hurt someone else or cause pain? Who wants to be embarrassed or humiliated? Who wants to make a mistake? NO ONE!

The quicker we identify our part, the quicker we release the baggage that begins to alter our true self and interferes with our potential. This does not mean that we always submit. This doesn't translate to being taken advantage of or abused. It means that YOU owe it to yourself to identify if your participation is the contention or selfishness and decide to do differently.

When the kids were little – neighbor kids too – I would call them together in a circle to discuss the conflict among the group. I told them that I would ask them a question that they had to answer. "What was your part in the situation, and who do you need to ask forgiveness from?" I didn't want to hear how someone else started it or what he or she said or did. I would randomly call on someone, maybe not even involved, and we would sit until each person identified his or her part, even to say, "I wasn't involved." We then asked for forgiveness and moved on to a great day – no lingering bad feelings – but resolve in each soul.

This is a great model for doing personal inventory. What is my part? If you begin to blame or do someone else's inventory

you risk losing another piece of personal growth. We don't always need to be right, but we have a right to be heard. Carry only what is yours and be free from chains that will bind you to another.

Mom Jay

YOUR THOUGHTS

POSITIVITY

"Turn that frown upside down." Unknown

When I was little and had my lower lip pushed out and my forehead scrunched to display my best mad face, my mom's favorite expression was, "Be careful, your face may freeze like that!" I wish I had heeded her advice, because I'm convinced it would have made many of my days happier... and also required less Botox in later years.

The truth in a smile is like magic. It can materialize out of nowhere, and it has the mystical ability to change not only your disposition but reach beyond yourself to others.

Try this little experiment the next time you catch yourself in a bad mood: First sit for a few seconds, acknowledge whatever has you in a funk and then decide to take control of your emotions. Then, consciously decide to smile. Do it even though it may feel forced. Do it even though it doesn't feel natural at first. Start picturing something that usually does make you smile (like playing with puppies or when your boyfriend surprises you with roses or that "A" you just got on your final exam). Here's the kicker: when you're smiling, it's next to impossible to be in a bad mood! Pretty soon, the smile will be genuine.

Practice smiling. Smile at yourself in the mirror. (Just the sight of you practicing like you're in a toothpaste commercial will make you smile). Not only are there scientific studies proving that smiling sets off all sorts of endorphins that are great for your mood, but smiling actually extends your lifespan. Happy people live longer. Smiling will not only have a positive impact on you, but it will make a shift in another person's day as well. Start paying attention to how people react when you smile at them. Some may find it awkward; smile anyway. Most will return the smile because it's contagious.

You have an unlimited number of smiles, and they don't cost a thing to give out. So do yourself and those you come in contact with a favor...smile like your life depends on it. Because it actually does!

Mom Rachel

Books: *E2* by Pam Grout and *Adventures in Manifesting* by Sarah Prout

YOUR THOUGHTS

POWER

You hear about leaders being "drunk with power." Instead, throughout my life, I've regarded power as something to be given away. You always have the power to love and to forgive. This is really the true test of character. It's not the easiest thing to do, but it's what defines pivotal moments in our lives. I came to this realization when I was a junior in college. I belonged to a big sorority and lived in the house along with 100 other girls.

I had an amazing group of friends, and for the most part I got along with everybody and everybody got along with me...everybody but a certain girl that we'll call Dorothy. She was a year older than I was and downright scary to me. She was strikingly gorgeous, and she knew it. She walked around campus as if people should be throwing rose petals in her wake. Dorothy had her own "mean girls" pack and on more than one occasion, I was at the receiving end of her snarky and disapproving comments and looks.

One particular day, I was being very rambunctious and loud, and she called me out on my behavior with a very public tongue lashing in front of 15 or so of our sorority sisters. I was mortified. If I could have disappeared spontaneously, I would have. This little incident turned my dislike of Dorothy into full-out disdain.

My tactic was to avoid her at all costs. My lying low worked until one fateful Tuesday night. I heard a knock on my door at close to midnight. I opened it to find none other than scary Dorothy. She was a contestant in a beauty pageant and "did not have a talent" for that portion of the contest. She continued to tell me that she had an artist costume and implored me to write her an inspirational monologue to go with her outfit about how life is art. I quickly responded with a resounding, "No," and I explained that I was studying for a test that I had in the morning. She left dejected, and I returned to my public relations book. But I couldn't study now. My mind was filled with thoughts about what was the right thing to do. On one hand, she needed my help. On the other hand, I had my own to do list to attend to, (not to mention, I was not a member of her fan club.) After I mulled it over, I pushed my book and notes aside and began to write a very eloquent and touching poem about how life is art. I handed the finished poem to her first thing in the morning.

She was shocked and elated, since I had declined to help her the night before. She went on to win in the pageant: her beauty and my brains.

The epiphany I had that night was that I had the power. I could have said yes or no. I could have forgiven or harbored bitterness. I could help or hurt another. My choice that day and ever since has been to try to rise above the hurt, always help an outreached hand and use my gifts for good.

I keep this story in the forefront of my mind. It has served me well in both business and my personal life countless times. It's empowering to give and be gracious, especially when it's least expected. We are all connected and our journey is love.

Mom Connie

YOUR THOUGHTS

PRAYER

"Do not be anxious about anything, but in everything, prayer and petition, with thanksgiving, present your requests to God. And the peace of God, which transcends all understanding, will guard your hearts and your minds in Christ Jesus." Philippians 4:6-7

Prayer is slowing down and quieting your mind to be with God.

It is hard because we all want to be self-reliant and independent. Prayer doesn't change God; it changes us. Through prayer God gives us peace that passes all understanding and strength to overcome. Prayer unlocks us to God's prevailing power, protection, and peace.

When we work, we work, but when we pray, God works. When prayer is weak, usually our faith is weak. When prayer becomes a habit, we stay continuously tuned to God's presence and open to receive his blessings. Prayer should be consistent, private, earnest, and specific.

The Bible shows us that authentic prayer includes:
- Worship   "Our Father who art in Heaven, hallowed by your name..."
- Submission   "Your will be done..."
- Requests   "Give us our daily bread..."
- Confession   "Forgive us our debts, as we forgive..."

Faith-filled prayers must focus on God not the issue and taking the first step to trust God.

God usually answers prayer in four ways:
- No   →   if the request is wrong
- Slow   →   if the timing is wrong
- Grow   →   if you are wrong
- Go   →   Right time, request, and you are right with God

Said another way, God answers prayer by saying yes, not now and/or I've got something even better for you.

Most importantly, we must trust God. He really knows best...I am most grateful for some unanswered prayers.

"My ways are higher... My thoughts are higher." Isaiah 55:8-9

Mom Connie

Book: *Too Busy Not to Pray* by Bill Hybels

YOUR THOUGHTS

RELATIONSHIPS

"A sweet friendship refreshes the soul." Proverbs 27:9

Yesterday I got a text that made my heart go pitter patter ... it was a life breathing text from a Godly friend that was covering me in prayer and had words of peace to share.

Do you have any of those friends? You know, those friends that are true friends?

God put me on a "friendship" journey a couple years ago, and I've learned so much and still am.

I want to be a Godly friend, a true friend ... a friend that stands the test of time ... not only do I want to be that type of friend, but I also want that type of friend. Not the surface friends but the deep friends ...

Have you ever wondered what a Godly friendship looks like?

When this all started, I noticed differences in relationships around me. I wanted more. But to have more, I knew it started with me. To have more, you have to be more. It's that whole we reap what we sow principle ... if you want friends, you have to be a friend. I got curious. What does a Godly friendship look like?

The Bible has lots to say about Godly friendships. Here are a few nuggets:

They CELEBRATE! Yes, they genuinely celebrate your accomplishments. Really celebrate. Not just lip service. I was convicted here. Why could I genuinely celebrate for some and not others? Because my heart wasn't right. Jealousy was playing a role in some relationships, and I needed some refining. There really isn't any place for jealousy in a God-breathed friendship. If the relationship is solid your accomplishments become your friends' accomplishments because more than likely you contributed to the success. Think about it: the prayers you poured over them, the support you provided, and even in some cases the accountability. All were massively important during the season leading up to their success and vice versa. Check out what the scripture says about jealousy: in James 3:14-15, "But if you have bitter jealousy and selfish ambition in your heart, do not be arrogant and so lie against the truth. This wisdom is not that which comes down from above, but is earthly, natural, and demonic." I've been here and know I will be here again; our flesh is weak, but that is where repenting comes into play. Confess and repent and watch God work.

They SPEAK TRUTH. This can be hard to do and hard to hear, but when it comes from a place of love, you know you have a keeper on your hands. Seriously, this is a friend you can trust to tell you things that are really for your own good, even if you may not want to hear it. This is a woman of prayer, and you know that she goes before God for you to seek wisdom on your behalf. She doesn't speak foolishly or simply to fill the air, she is intentional with her words and holds you to the fire when you've acted out of character. Oh man, I cherish the ladies in my life that play this role. And it works both ways. Who are you praying over, seeking wisdom for, and speaking intentional words over?

Brethren, if any person is overtaken in misconduct or sin of any sort, you who are spiritual [who are responsive to and controlled by the Spirit] should set him right and restore and reinstate him, without any sense of superiority and with all gentleness. (Galatians 6:1) Did you catch that? No superiority.

GOSSIP FREE ZONE: Godly friends aren't gossips. Eeeek, I was super convicted in this area. I gossiped way too much. I needed major refinement here. The Bible has a TON to say about gossipers. Can you comfortably share something with your friend and know without a doubt that your conversation will stay private? True friends are honest and trustworthy with matters of the heart. A real friend will defend you in public and confront you in private. They have your back and stand up for you when you aren't around. Do you do that for anybody or do you fall right into the gossip trap? Check out what Proverbs 20:19 has to say about gossip: whoever goes around as a gossip tells secrets. Do not associate with a person whose mouth is always open.

GIVER: Godly friends are givers. They freely share their gifts with the world and are quick to give to their friends. Both parties give sacrificially without hesitation. Did you catch both? It's a give and take, not just a take. Sacrifices are made in these relationships. I admit I have sacrificed some sleep to sit up with a crying girlfriend or have missed scheduled appointments because a friend was in need, and so have others for me. Friends who take from theirs to give to ours – these are the most treasured friendships.

"Greater love has no one than this: that someone lay down his life for his friends." (John 15:13)

Who is refreshing your soul? I'm so grateful for the friends in my life that refresh my soul, and I love surprises like the one I received yesterday. A heartfelt text from a Godly friend definitely refreshed my soul and immediately brought peace.

If you feel like you're lacking here, it starts with YOU. Work on being a better friend and you'll start to attract the exact same thing!

Mom Jenny

Book: *The Holy Bible*

YOUR THOUGHTS

RESILIENCE

"Do not judge me by my success, judge me by how many times I fell down and got back up again." Nelson Mandela

We are born with a natural instinct to be resilient; it is up to us to cultivate that trait or weaken it. As children, we learn to talk, walk, and try new things despite initial and multiple setbacks. As we grow older, we experience disappointments and challenges during our educational journeys, and in our personal and professional lives. We need to equip ourselves with tools that allow us to successfully manage hardships and move on.

As a mom, it is hard sometimes to balance the desire to protect my daughter from discomfort and pain, and allowing her to experience it and using those moments as learning milestones. Normally, my first instinct is to shield her from pain and to intervene on her behalf. Although, this is more rewarding in the short term, the consequences may weaken her ability to deal effectively with future challenges.

In her sophomore year, my daughter had a difficult class. When I was on an international trip, she called me crying that the course was too hard and she planned to drop it. My heart ached for her, and I wanted to support her decision. However, I was thinking that this was an opportunity for her to learn how to handle difficult situations.

Having asked her not to drop the class, I needed to let her know that there were tools at her disposal that would allow her to overcome the difficulty of the class. That is when our journey with resilience began. I encouraged her to find online resources, offered extra help, and found resources that could be useful in reducing her stress. Slowly but steadily, she became self-reliant and ended the year well.

My intention was to teach my daughter with love and guidance to be resilient and manage a challenge that caused her a lot of discomfort.

My wish is the same for you. Welcome challenges and with resilience overcome them.

Mom Aisha

YOUR THOUGHTS

RIGOR

Do not mistake aggression for rigor, for you can have one without the other. On the surface, rigor can look timid or rigor can look assertive. Many of the definitions of rigor involve harshness and rigidity but I choose to look at rigor as it is often used in educational settings. Rigor involves pushing yourself beyond where it is easy. If you are employing rigor, your task should feel difficult. It means that you are pushing yourself beyond what is comfortable and you may feel uneasy. It will be up to you to make friends with those feelings that arise due to employing rigor. But remember, rigor also involves maintaining balance. It is okay to do things that feel comfortable, not to always push yourself or be at the learning edge. However, you don't want to get overly complacent. Rigor helps you continue to learn and grow.

At my age, I am working to maintain some rigor in physical activity. It means if I walk or hike, I do so at an incline so that my heart rate goes up a bit, and I feel a little out of breath. This pushes me just enough so that my body is tired. If I go to an aerobics class, I lift my knees and sweat so my heart gets some exercise here, too. After class I feel invigorated but later that evening I feel exhausted and sometimes cranky. This I know to be the price of rigor for me.

Rigor is a life lesson for me. For some people, rigor comes naturally. They love the idea of pushing themselves to and beyond their limits. They embrace the growing edge and thrive on the search for excellence. While I deeply appreciate these traits, my natural inclination is to chill out. I love easy days of summer and staying comfortable. However, within the last decade, I have come to appreciate the by-products of rigor:

increased self-esteem and self-efficacy, the ability to do things I never thought possible, cultivation of persistence, patience, and tenacity. These are traits that will also add value to your life. I also am learning that I do not have to give up chilling and staying comfortable. They just need to be coupled with healthy rigor. So make friends with rigor, and it will serve you well throughout your life.

Mom Natalie

YOUR THOUGHTS

RISK TAKING

"A ship in harbor is safe, but that is not what ships are built for." John A. Shedd

While you are young, take risks.

Take the trip to the country you are curious about but are second guessing because you don't know the language. There's an app for that! Take the job offer that you are scared that you might not be ready for, because most likely, you are. If you are not, you'll learn swiftly. Take the class to learn to paint or kickbox. Write the book; ask the person out; launch your startup. It's in the areas where you step out of your comfort zone that you will grow the most. Do it now! Don't delay, because the offers that come your way may have a short shelf-life, or others who are willing to take the risk will be the ones who reap the rewards.

The only thing worse than failing is having regret about not doing the things that you are dreaming about.

Mom Rachel

YOUR THOUGHTS

SELF-ESTEEM

"You are altogether beautiful, my love; there is no flaw in you." Song of Solomon 4:7

You Are Worth It!

Some days it is a struggle to feel good about yourself. There is so much pressure to look and act a certain way. You may feel that you are never enough for this world: pretty enough, thin enough, smart enough, popular enough. But you are always enough in the Lord's eyes. You are "God's handiwork" (Ephesians 2:10), and His opinion is the only one that matters.

When you begin to see yourself through the eyes of God, you will find that you can love and respect yourself just as He loves and respects you. It is not easy to overcome the outside voices and pressures, but choose to listen to the Lord instead. "Fear not, for I am with you; be not dismayed, for I am your God; I will strengthen you, I will help you, I will uphold you with my righteous right hand." (Isaiah 41:10)

By sending His only Son to die on the cross, God showed His absolute love for you. Through this ultimate sacrifice, you can be assured that He believes you are worthy! Keep Him close and rely on His love to help provide you with the strength and confidence to help you succeed in life's journey. "I will praise you because I have been remarkably and wonderfully made. Your works are wonderful, I know this very well." (Psalm 139:14)

Never forget, you are precious and possess immeasurable value. You are worth it!

Mom Mary Kay

YOUR THOUGHTS

SERENITY

"Jesus responded, 'Why are you so afraid? You have so little faith!" Matthew 8:26

Serenity is a state of peace that comes from within. It comes from a knowing that all is well. With Jesus, there is not only calm, but great calm. This tells me that I can trust Jesus and have faith no matter what challenges arise; He is my source of inner tranquility.

God grant me the serenity to accept the things I cannot change (circumstances), the courage to change the thing I can (attitude, actions), and the wisdom to know the difference. Living an untroubled life is not realistic, as troubles are part of life. However, we can be thankful that through God we can find tranquility in the midst of difficulties.

"All who listen to me will live in peace, untroubled by fear or harm." Proverbs 1:33

Mom Gina

YOUR THOUGHTS

SERVICE

"The best way to find yourself is to lose yourself in the service of others." Mahatma Gandhi

How many times have you been asked, "What do you want to be when you grow up?" It seems innocent enough. When you were younger, it seemed so easy to come up with one, two, or many ideas on what you wanted to be when you were an adult. As you mature and go through school and on to college, your idea of what you want to be may change. Your decision may be shaped by the necessary criteria needed to obtain that degree and pursue your chosen profession. Required entrance exams, extended schooling, and monetary obligations may influence your decision.

What if you don't know what you want to do with your life? Or what if you get into a profession that you do not enjoy? You may feel lost or confused. You are so focused on your decisions, your challenges, and the "what ifs" that you have a hard time on focusing. It becomes easy to be consumed with your own problems that you are so weighed down you cannot see beyond yourself.

If you find yourself questioning your purpose in life, remember this quote by Gandhi: "When you decide to give of yourself to help others and focus on their problems or needs, you free your mind of your own troubles. Whether you volunteer or choose a profession that serves mankind even if only for a time, a person gains a different perspective as to what is truly important in life. There is no cause nobler than the giving of yourself with time, effort, spirit, enthusiasm, care, kindness, and compassion to help others. You will be

contributing to the betterment of the world, and in turn, you will find yourself and what you truly love. You will obtain a clarity to make clear decisions and will value life, people, and community more dearly. Things that seemed so confusing and complex before will make sense and decisions will be easier to make."

Mom Sharin

YOUR THOUGHTS

SIGNIFICANCE

If you are fortunate, there are people in your life that without them you would not be the same. They save you, believe in you, lift you up and make sure you have an abundant life of love.

For me these angels are my sisters, Carolyn and Cathy. They are fifteen and sixteen years older than I am and have been part mom-part sister. Throughout my life they have cared for me and shaped my values, principles, and choices. I actually lived with each of them at different times. They both gave unconditional love and spent countless hours and endless resources to ensure that I grew up healthy and happy.

On Easter 2017, my beautiful, talented, and feisty sister, Cathy, passed away. By God's grace, my older sister, Carolyn, and I were together. We had come to visit Cathy and found her in very bad health. In typical "Cooper girl" form, we jumped into action to ensure Cathy had the proper care in a loving place. We would not stop until our sweet sister, who was in pain and suffering had the best care in the entire area. You see we were the dynamic trio. Nothing and no one could stop us when we were together.

The night before Cathy went to heaven, she told Carolyn and me that she felt so "happy, peaceful, and loved." Typical Cathy – leaving just in time to make a big party (Easter in heaven), ensuring Carolyn and I were together as support, and only when she knew that we both would be okay without her.

The year before, I had sent Cathy a book that had changed my life, *Search for Significance* by the inspiring and wonderful Geri Marr Burdman. I wrote on the cover to her: "Never doubt your significance in my life and my daughter's." A story for another time...but you see, Cathy saved both of our lives with her gifts and generosity. Sadly, Cathy's husband had passed a few years before, and she didn't have any children of her own. Despite being a nurse that had saved multiple lives and a renowned artist, Cathy was doubting her purpose and significance in this stage of her life.

After she passed away, we found the book *Search for Significance* that I had sent her in a prominent place within reach. The following handwritten note was folded in half marking one of her favorite passages.

This I believe in 100 Words...

God does not make mistakes.

I have been and still am loved.

We all have a purpose.

To learn more – listen.

Be still and know that I am God.

I am blessed every day.

Live your authentic self in love and peace to create grace and wisdom.

The more you give, the more you get.

To love unconditionally is hard, but freeing.

For every negative, there is always a positive somewhere.

When you are at your most down – reach out and give to someone.

The sun will rise and set every day.

There is good in this world.

Heaven is a place of complete understanding.

My parents did the best they could with what they had at the time.

My sisters would go to bat for me whether I am right or wrong.

God has a sense of humor.

Forgiveness is more for yourself than others.

Never doubt your significance. My sister's agape love – a beautiful overflowing love which seeks nothing in return – changed my life forever.

Mom Connie

Book: *Search for Significance* by Geri Marr Burdman

YOUR THOUGHTS

STEWARDSHIP

I believe that the joy, depth, and quality of your life will be greatly enhanced if you understand that ownership is an illusion. You do not own your body. You do not own land. You do not own your dog. Parents do not own their children. You are a steward of them all. If you make this one shift in thinking – from ownership to stewardship – you will make decisions that are kinder, gentler, more sustainable and that will bring you more joy and satisfaction.

You will realize that everything in this lifetime is transient and precious. You become a steward of our land, oceans, and relationships. Imagine if we all realized that we are stewards of the rainforest. For this brief period of time that we are on this planet, we are entrusted with caring for it, loving it, and passing it along to the next generation of stewards.

There are groups of people, like our indigenous brothers and sisters, who understood this innately. Our modern society has much to learn from this way of life. I constantly challenge myself to be a good steward of my body. I don't always succeed. I don't always feed it the most nourishing foods, have it move in ways that are joyful, but I am learning. Like all lessons worth learning and living, I believe that stewardship is a lifelong one.

You may believe that you own the goods you purchase, but that too is an illusion. If you purchase an item from the mall, you have made an exchange, and it is your responsibility to care for it with respect, know its value, and even pass it along to someone else if it is time. It is easier to exploit someone or something, to exercise power over it, if you believe you own it. You can look back on many examples of this in history.

Be conscious when people are trying to exercise power over you, consciously or unconsciously. If this happens consistently and continuously, then you have a decision to make. Do you stay in the situation, leave, or try to change it?

Work to be a steward and to see stewardship in its many forms as often as possible. I have worked your whole life to be the best parent-steward I can be. I understand that I do not own you or our relationship but I work every day to nurture and value them. My hope is that you grow your own stewardship with life.

Mom Natalie

YOUR THOUGHTS

STRENGTH

We all want to be self-reliant and independent, but asking for help is not a sign of weakness.

Quite the opposite in fact. I spent the majority of my life polishing the "S" on my chest and wearing my super hero cape with pride. From a very young age I can remember reciting the same mantra over and over again: "I can do it myself!" I bellowed with my hands on my hips. Even during times when I rationally knew that my parents, friends, or coworkers might have some guidance for me that could make what I was working on so much easier and cut my learning curve in half, their advice fell on deaf ears. I had convinced myself that to accept their help would make me appear like I was weak and somehow deficient.

Fast forward four decades, (yes, I'm a slow learner,) and I found myself facing a divorce, and I was truly at a point where I felt my life was unraveling. I had hit rock bottom.

It was the first time in my life when I started to accept the help my friends and family were offering. They rallied around me and helped me do physical things like repaint my house to get it ready for sale, helped me move, and even watched my kids so that I could have an adult night out to save my sanity – or what was left of it.

Now, I can so clearly see that accepting people's help when it's extended is not a sign of weakness but one of strength and humility. It is proclaiming to the world (or at a minimum to yourself,) that you don't have all the answers. Quite possibly others who have walked in your shoes just might have some wisdom and support to lend. I also saw that friends truly do want to help or they would not have offered. A friend wants to feel needed, so as much as you might resist receiving someone's gift of time, talent, or treasure, it ends up being a blessing to both the giver and the recipient.

Yes, I'm a recovering perfectionist that thought I had to do everything myself. Today, I can freely admit I am perfectly imperfect and that my friends who are there by my side knew that all along and love me regardless.

Mom Rachel

YOUR THOUGHTS

THE GOLDEN RULE

The universality of the Golden Rule across world religions is prevalent and profound. It is the foundation of the essence of community.

Christianity

All things whatsoever ye would that men should do to you, do ye so to them; for this is the law and the prophets.

Matthew 7:1

Confucianism

Do not do to others what you would not like yourself. Then there will be no resentment against you, either in the family or in the state.

Analects 12:2

Buddhism

Hurt not others in ways that you yourself would find hurtful.

Udana-Varga 5,1

Hinduism

This is the sum of duty; do naught onto others what you would not have them do unto you.

Mahabharata 5,1517

Islam   *No one of you is a believer until he desires for his brother that which he desires for himself.*

Sunnah

Judaism   *What is hateful to you, do not do to your fellowman. This is the entire Law; all the rest is commentary.*

Talmud, Shabbat 3id

Taoism   *Regard your neighbor's gain as your gain, and your neighbor's loss as your own loss.*

Tai Shang Kan Yin P'ien

Zoroastrianism   *That nature alone is good which refrains from doing another whatsoever is not good for itself.*

Dadisten-I-dinik, 94,5

Mom Rachel

YOUR THOUGHTS

TRUTH

"... and you will know the truth, and the truth will set you free." John 8:32 ESV

Truth is seldom recognized and often despised, yet it is the essence of God, the foundation of our character, and the cornerstone of trust in every meaningful relationship.

This I know: God and God's word are the only absolute truth – the alpha and the omega, the beginning and the end. So, why is it we often see or believe different truths? Do our bias and own paradigms blind us? Who is right and who is wrong?

A great example of this is the parable of the blind men and the elephant. It goes something like this:

In a distant village, a long time ago, there lived six blind men. One day the villagers announced, "Hey, there is an elephant in the village today." They had never seen or felt an elephant before and so decided, "Even though we would not be able to see it, let us go and feel it anyway." And thus they went down to the village to touch and feel the elephant to learn what animal this was, and they described it as follows:

By Itcho Hanabusa 1888

"Hey, the elephant is a pillar," said the first man who touched his leg.

"Oh, no! It is like a rope," argued the second after touching the tail.

"Oh, no! It is like a thick branch of a tree," the third man spouted after touching the trunk.

"It is like a big hand fan" said the fourth man feeling the ear.

"It is like a huge wall," sounded the fifth man, who groped the belly.

"It is like a solid pipe," said the sixth man with the tusk in his hand.

They all fell into heated argument as to who was right in describing the big beast, all sticking to their own perception. A wise sage happened to hear the argument, stopped, and asked them, "What is the matter?" They said, "We cannot agree to what the elephant is like."

The wise man then calmly said, "Each one of you is correct, and each one of you is wrong. Because each one of you touched only a part of the elephant's body. Thus you only have a partial view of the animal. If you put your partial views together, you will get an idea of what an elephant looks like."

The parable of the blind men and the elephant is used to illustrate how biases can blind us, preventing us from seeking a more complete understanding of the nature of things.

Often our interpretation of the facts of a situation can be influenced or distorted based on our own experiences and the filter through which we view the world. So, it is with an open heart and caution that we should listen and clarify, before assuming.

Speaking truth can be difficult and have challenging consequences. Yet, what is the alternative? Lies lead to more lies. Small compromises in truth or honesty can lead to big consequences. Once you lose trust, it is nearly impossible to regain it completely. Integrity is the one attribute that no one can take from you, but that you can give away by not being true to yourself.

Honesty is being free from deception. Trust is built by honesty. It is the glue that holds relationships together.

*"**We see** the **world,** not as it is, but as **we** are – or, as **we** are conditioned to **see** it."* Stephen Covey

Mom Connie

Book: *Seven Habits of Highly Effective People*
by Stephen Covey

YOUR THOUGHTS

WISDOM

"For the Lord gives wisdom, and from his mouth comes knowledge and understanding." Proverbs 2:6

I don't remember not being a Christian. I was born into a Christian family and grew up knowing Jesus Christ as my Savior. I admit in the past I may have wandered away at times from my relationship with Jesus, and I didn't always put as much time as I should have into growing closer to him, but even then, I don't ever recall a time in my life without Jesus in my heart. With Jesus in my heart, I always know I can turn to him if I need wisdom.

When I was growing up, I often thought of God giving me wisdom like a flashing green light or a red light on a signal. If God wanted me to go do something I envisioned a green light flashing "yes," and if he didn't, I envisioned a red light flashing "no." But it isn't really like that. Seeking God's wisdom means getting to know Him and the many wise role models He tells us about and the many examples He describes to us in the Bible.

Today, as a wife and mother of two young children, I study God's word, the Bible, and pray every day; sometimes I talk to God all day! The reason I do this is because I know I need wisdom from God to help me along the way. There are many times when I really need God's wisdom to help me know what to do, especially when I am faced with big decisions for my family or for me. I rely on His teaching in the Bible and trust Him to show me what to do, because I honestly don't always know what is best for us. But God does! God will give us wisdom when we trust Him. He is the source of wisdom and will give it to us if we ask for it. Our job is to trust Him and to be willing to act when He does give us the wisdom we need.

Three Wise Moms

"If any of you lacks wisdom, you should ask God, who gives generously to all without finding fault, and it will be given to you." James: 1:5

Mom Karen

Book: *The Holy Bible*

YOUR THOUGHTS

WORSHIP

"But just as your body needs sleep, your soul needs time to rest in God. Craig Groeschel

As a child, my grandmother told me a story about prayers that shaped the way I think about God.

A new bride living with her husband and in-laws always disappeared at time of prayers, (Muslims pray five times a day). Her new family became suspicious, and her husband decided to spy on her. He followed her as she left the house for the garden and stood next to a tree. He watched as she made the prayer movements: standing, bowing, prostrating, and sitting. As she moved, the trees were imitating her movements as if they were praying with her, the stones were repeating her words as if worshiping with her. Her husband was stunned. When she was done, he asked her why she was praying alone and what she was reciting in her prayers. She explained that she never had learned the verses in the Quran she needed for prayers, and she was embarrassed to pray in front of her new family. She said only, "God is great," throughout her prayer. Her husband taught her how to pray properly, and she was able to join the others at times of prayer, but no trees or stones prayed with her.

The moral of the story is that God looks into our heart while people judge us based on external rituals. When the new bride did not know how to pray, her love for God and desire to worship overcame her inability to recite the prayers correctly. Her desire was pure and not based on learned rituals; that is why the universe prayed with her. Many people of faith pray and recite the words of God, but that is not translated into action and behaviors. Worship is about having God in our hearts to guide our interactions with people and our environment. It is not about going to houses of worship for congregational prayer. It feels as if we are all schizophrenic; we pray and praise God at times of prayers, then leave God and carry on with our lives as if God lives only in places of worship.

I once read a book by the Hindu philosopher Tagore. In one of the short stories, he describes a king who built a temple of gold and invited the most learned Hindu sage to come and teach in it. When the sage arrived, he refused to teach in the temple and decided to preach under a tree. The king was furious. The sage said to the king, "You burdened the locals with heavy taxes to build this temple transgressing God's laws; God loves and cares about people and God certainly does not need a golden temple."

A dear Christian friend once asked me how I know when God is present; I realized then that God is always present in my heart, except that I am too busy most of the time to recognize that. God is in the air we breathe and in the leaves of the trees. God is in the sun that warms us and in the moon that lights our dark nights. God is everywhere and most importantly, God is in our hearts.

Mom Aisha

YOUR THOUGHTS

YOUR STORY

Many times in your life you will look around and see that people have it together. You will notice that "everyone" seems happy, or that his or her life is perfect. We have in our heads a plan that tells us life must follow a certain protocol, and if it doesn't, somehow we have failed. Wouldn't it be great to reframe our thinking to looking for unique journeys and how each person finds their way throughout a lifetime?

Let us learn by watching from a different perspective. As you walk your path, embrace it. Each step is yours; no one has ever walked where you walk. People have walked beside you and you might learn from them, or you might decide to look away. You might even watch more closely. You are in charge.

Not everyone walks the same, but in the end everyone finishes with their own story. Write yours!

Mom Jay

YOUR THOUGHTS

AFTERWORD:

Families are the compass that guides us.
They are the inspiration to reach great heights,
and our comfort when we occasionally falter.
– Brad Henry

This book of guidance has been developed by many wise moms to give their children a compass to use as they enter their next phase of life. The moms understand there are differences in each family, but their wisdom allowed them to see and recognize their shared values and goals.

This guide reminds each child what they have been taught:

Honor God in all things you do. Listen to and follow the voice deep in your heart.

Serve and help others. When you serve others it makes you a better person. You shift from "me thinking" to a "we thinking." It helps you see and use your gifts to make a difference and see our interconnections in the world. Become instruments of a greater order and goodness.

Grow together in your faith. Growing in your faith and knowledge will keep you on the right path and allow you to be what you were meant to be in your life.

Share your story and gifts with others. When you share, you define yourself. Make sure you speak encouraging and helpful things to others. You become what you speak and do.

Written by Carolyn Spooner

FINAL THOUGHTS